The World of Mythology:

Mayan and Aztec Mythology

By Jim Ollhoff

Visit us at
WWW.ABDOPUBLISHING.COM

Printed in the United States of America, North Mankato, Minnesota.
012011
092011

 PRINTED ON RECYCLED PAPER

Editor: John Hamilton
Graphic Design: Sue Hamilton
Cover Design: Neil Klinepier
Cover Photo: Gonzalo Ordóñez
Interior Photos and Illustrations: Alamy-pgs 12 & 14; AP-pgs 16, 19, 21 & 28; Corbis-pgs 5, 15, 18, 20 & 27; Getty Images-pgs 4 & 24; Glow Images-pgs 11, 14, 22, 23, 25, 26 & 29; Granger Collection-pg 27; iStockphoto-border image; Kmusser-pg 6; National Geographic-pg 8; Photo Researchers-pgs 7 & 9; Thinkstock-pgs 17, 31 & 32.

Library of Congress Cataloging-in-Publication Data

Ollhoff, Jim, 1959-
  Mayan and Aztec mythology / Jim Ollhoff.
    p. cm. -- (The world of mythology)
  ISBN 978-1-61714-724-1
  1. Maya mythology--Juvenile literature. 2. Aztec mythology--Juvenile literature. I. Title.
  F1435.3.R3O45 2011
  972.81--dc22
                                2010042976

CONTENTS

The Mighty Myth..4

The World of the Mayans...6

The Soul of the Mayans..8

The Mayan Creation: The Popol Vuh..................................10

Popular Mayan Gods...12

The End of the World in 2012?..16

The World of the Aztecs...18

The Soul of the Aztecs..20

The Aztec Foundation Story..22

Popular Aztec Gods...24

Why Did the Aztecs Fall? 28

Glossary...30

Index...32

THE MIGHTY MYTH

The sun had set, and the Mayan people of Central America gathered by the bonfire. There, amidst the flickering light and crackling wood, people told stories. Some of the stories were about the challenges of the day's hunt, and the spiritual forces that were with the hunters. Other stories explained why the animals behaved as they did. There were stories revealing why the sun went down, or why the moon is in the sky. As the people sat around the fire, some told stories about how people first got fire from the gods.

This scene has played out thousands of ways, in thousands of places, throughout history, and not just for the Mayans and the Aztecs. When the sun went down, and people could no longer do their chores, they met by the fire. There, they told stories. The stories were about life, the gods, and the universe. Parents told the stories to their children. The children grew up and told the stories to their children.

Telling stories has always been important to people. People of all cultures, in every part of the world, tell stories. Some stories teach important life lessons. Others explain natural processes. Stories can even give comfort or guidance in hard times.

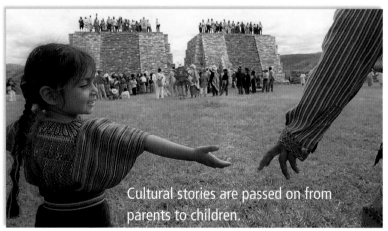
Cultural stories are passed on from parents to children.

The people of Central America and other cultures told stories about spiritual forces that explained why things happened in the world.

THE WORLD OF THE MAYANS

The Mayans were a collection of peoples in Central America. They came from many city-states and spoke several languages, and they formed a loose association beginning about 200 AD. Their lands included parts of

Red Outlined Area= Mayan Civilization

present-day Mexico, Guatemala, Honduras, and the Yucatán Peninsula.

The Mayans are remembered for their pyramids, temples, and huge stone sculptures. They were very advanced in astronomy and mathematics as well. They had a very intricate writing system, with thousands of books. Unfortunately, almost all of those books have been lost, so our knowledge of the Mayan people is incomplete.

The Mayan civilization declined quickly after about 900 AD. The reasons for the decline are unclear, but probably were the result of at least two things. The Mayan civilization was weakened by constant warfare. There was also a long drought that resulted in severe food shortages. Great Mayan cities were abandoned as people migrated to other areas and joined neighboring tribes.

There are still Mayans today, in Mexico and Guatemala. They still speak their ancestral language and try to uphold some of the culture of their ancestors.

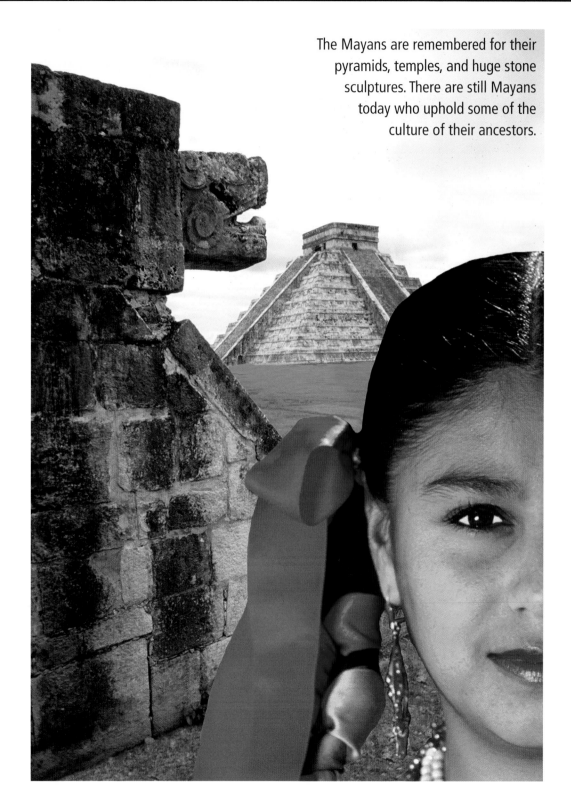

The Mayans are remembered for their pyramids, temples, and huge stone sculptures. There are still Mayans today who uphold some of the culture of their ancestors.

THE SOUL OF THE MAYANS

Mayan mythology is very complicated. There were hundreds of gods. Many of them had four different personalities, to coincide with the four directions—north, south, east, and west. Many of the gods had two natures, such as appearing as both young and old, or male and female. Many gods had the same or similar functions as other gods.

When someone died a natural death, Mayans believed that the dead person went into one of the nine layers of Xibalba, the Mayan underworld. Each layer of Xibalba had gods who ruled that particular layer, with names like Flying Scab, Gathered Blood, and Pus Demon. If a person died a violent death, such as in warfare, they could go to heaven. The Mayan heaven had 13 layers, all with particular gods who ruled the various levels.

Temples were usually built on top of mountains or pyramids. In this way, the people could be closer to heaven.

Mayan temples were sometimes built on top of pyramids, such as El Castillo at Chichen Itza in Mexico.

Above: The Mayans believed that if a person died a violent death, such as in warfare, they could go to heaven.

THE MAYAN CREATION: THE POPOL VUH

The Mayan creation story was written in a book called the Popol Vuh. When the Spanish took over Central America in the early 1500s, they outlawed the book and destroyed every copy they could find. However, a few books survived. They were then copied by Mayan priests, who blended their own mythology with Spanish Catholicism.

The Popol Vuh said that two groups of gods wanted to create people. However, it took them a while to do this. First, they made animals, but then realized that the animals couldn't talk or give the gods respect. Then the gods tried to make humans out of mud, but that didn't work either. They tried to make humans out of wood, but that just produced people who had no feelings or thoughts.

The Popol Vuh then tells stories of how the gods battled each other. Finally, people were created out of corn, and given the purpose of respecting the gods and sacrificing to them.

Mayans believed they were created out of corn.

Above: A statue of the Mayan maize god. The statue's headdress is a stylized ear of corn and his hair is shown as corn silk. The Mayan stories in the Popol Vuh book tell how the gods created humans out of yellow and white corn.

POPULAR MAYAN GODS

ayans had a creator god and a god of death. They also had gods who exhibited power and strength. Popular Mayan gods included:

Itzamna:
Itzamna was a creator god who lived in the sky, and was the master of day and night. Despite his power, he was usually pictured as a toothless old man. He gave humans writing, religion, medicine, and the calendar.

Itzamna

Ah Puch:

Like a grim reaper, Ah Puch collected the souls of those who had just died. He was pictured as a skeleton, or with a skull head and a corpse as a body.

Ah Puch

Chac: Chac was the gentle rain god, who was sometimes pictured as a reptile with long fangs and wide eyes. Chac's tears formed rain. Generally, Chac was a friendly god who brought corn to the people of Earth.

Kinich-Ahau: He was the sun god during the day, and he ruled the underworld at night. He was pictured as a jaguar at night, the most powerful of the Central American cats. Mayan priests wore the skins of jaguars to show their power.

Pauahtun: This god appeared in four different ways, holding up the sky at the four corners of the world. He was also the god of thunder and wind. Because he was drunk much of the time, the thunder and wind were unpredictable and sometimes deadly.

THE END OF THE WORLD IN 2012?

The Mayan calendar stopped in 2012, much the same way our calendars stop on December 31. We don't believe the world will end on December 31, and the Mayans didn't believe that the world would end in 2012.

The Mayans actually used several calendars, which they believed were brought to humans by the god Itzamna. They used the Tzolk'in Calendar, a 260-day calendar that helped them know when to plant crops. They also used the Haab Calendar, which was 360 days, followed by a 5-day waiting period. But the Mayans also wanted a longer calendar to record things that happened over many centuries. So, they created the Long Count Calendar. This was a calendar that repeated every 5125 years. The first cycle of the Long Count Calendar ends in the year 2012 of our calendar.

Several books and Hollywood movies have used the idea that the world will end in 2012. However, the Mayans never said or believed that. In fact, they believed that the end of each cycle should be a time of great rejoicing and celebration.

Modern Mayans celebrate the new year.

Above: The Mayan calendar stopped in 2012, but that was just the end of the Long Count Calendar. They did not think the world would end in 2012.

THE WORLD OF
THE AZTECS

few hundred years after the Mayans, another association of people began to emerge. They founded the city of Tenochtitlán about 1325 AD, and this became the capital of the Aztec Empire. Some historians date the start of the Aztec Empire to 1427, with the merger of three large city-states, which came together for support and protection. The land of the Aztecs was mostly located in today's southern Mexico.

The Aztecs were expert farmers. They cultivated many crops with complex irrigation systems. By 1500 AD, there may have been as many as six million people in the Aztec Empire.

Right: A bustling marketplace at the Aztec capital city of Tenochtitlán.

Left: The Spanish armies under Hernán Cortés brought superior weapons and horses to defeat the Aztecs. However, it was the Spanish army's unknown weapon of the smallpox virus that destroyed up to half the native Aztec population.

The world of the Aztecs came to an abrupt end starting in 1519 with the invasion of the Spanish armies under Hernán Cortés. In 1521, the capital of the Aztecs was destroyed. The Spanish army was much smaller than the Aztec army. But the Spanish had a weapon that they didn't even realize they had brought with them: smallpox. Historians say that it's possible that up to half the population of the Aztecs contracted the dreaded and often fatal disease. The superior weapons of the Spanish, going against a decimated and weakened Aztec population, brought about the end of the Aztec Empire.

The Soul of the Aztecs

The Aztecs believed that the gods needed human blood to survive and to perform their tasks. While earlier civilizations also performed human sacrifice, the Aztecs are most famous for it. Sacrificial humans were often prisoners of war. They were killed by having their hearts removed. The Aztecs believed that a victim's soul went straight to Tonatiuhichan, the Place of the Sun.

One Aztec myth tells the story of how the universe was created. The creator gods, Quetzalcoatl and Tezcatlipoca, killed a giant monster, and then cut her in two. Half of her body became the sky, and the other half of her body became the Earth. Crops, plants, and trees grew out of her body. The myth says that this monster could be heard at night, screaming for human hearts to eat. If she were fed, she would continue to provide crops from her body.

While some other cultures around the world practiced human sacrifice, it seems that few other cultures did it as much as the Aztecs. In fact, the Aztecs often fought wars not with the intent to kill people, but to capture them so that the prisoners could be used as human sacrifices to the gods.

An Aztec mask with a skull and sacrificial knife.

Above: Aztecs sacrificed humans believing that the gods needed the blood to survive.

THE AZTEC FOUNDATION STORY

ztec myths say that the founders of their people came down from the north, from a place called Aztlan, which is where the word *Aztec* comes from. Historians have tried to determine if Aztlan was a real place or not. In the 1830s, a man in Wisconsin discovered an indian burial ground, and proclaimed that it must be Aztlan. More likely, the forerunners of the Aztecs wandered out of northern and central Mexico, when an earlier civilization called the Toltecs broke apart.

So, the Aztec myth is probably true. The people who would become the Aztecs really did come down from the north. A myth said that they had to find an eagle, a symbol of the Aztec war god. When they found the eagle god, he told them to settle where they stood, on an island on Lake Texcoco. There, they built the city called Tenochtitlán. The modern capital of Mexico City was built up around the ruins of Tenochtitlán. In fact, many of the streets in Mexico City still follow the streets that the Aztecs built in Tenochtitlán.

An eagle on an Aztec temple.

Above: A museum model and an illustration of the city of Tenochtitlán. According to myth, the original Aztec people came from the north. When they found an eagle god, he told them to settle where they stood. This was an island on Lake Texcoco.

POPULAR AZTEC GODS

The Aztecs were strong worshippers and followers of a powerful creation god, as well as gods and goddesses of the elements.

Quetzalcoatl:

The Aztecs, like many cultures, combined the mythology of defeated tribes into their own. A feathered serpent god had been worshiped in Central American cultures for centuries, but under the Aztecs, Quetzalcoatl became one of the most widely worshipped Aztec gods. According to the myth, he helped create the world, he brought learning, and he gave corn to humanity. He was the patron god of priests and rulers.

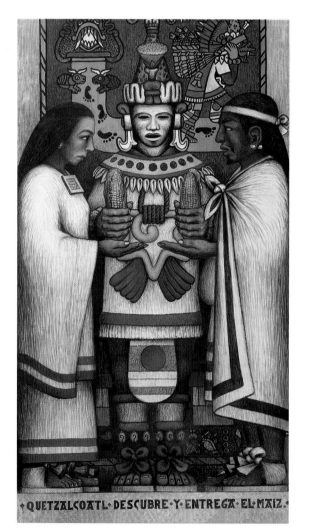

Right: A mural showing Quetzalcoatl giving corn to humans.

QUETZALCOATL·DESCUBRE·Y·ENTREGA·EL·MAIZ·

Xolotl:

He was the twin brother of Quetzalcoatl, but he usually took the appearance of a deformed dog. People could pray to him, but if his ears were facing the wrong way, he couldn't hear them. He grew to dislike people, and caused hardships and troubles for humanity. He had a number of jobs, including being the god of bad luck, the god of fire, and the protector of the sun at nighttime.

A statue of Xolotl, the twin brother of Quetzalcoatl.

Tezcatlipoca:

Another brother of Quetzalcoatl, he was the god of sun and harvest, but also the god of war and death. Tezcatlipoca behaved one way and then later would behave another way. He was called the Lord of the Smoking Mirror because he had a mirror in which he could see the future. He sometimes took the form of a jaguar.

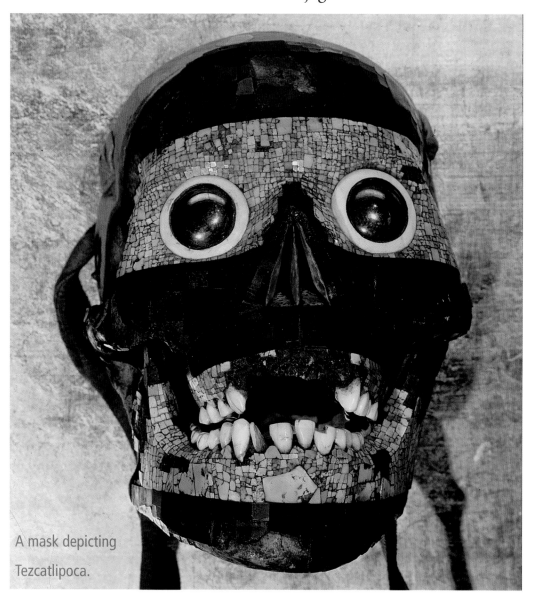

A mask depicting Tezcatlipoca.

Chalchiuhtlicue

Chalchiuhtlicue:

This was the goddess of rivers, lakes, and water. Her name means Woman of the Jade Skirt. She was the protector of children and the protector of women giving birth. When she was angry, she could create hurricanes.

Tlaloc

Tlaloc:

Aztecs depended on rain to keep the crops growing, so they had several gods who oversaw rain and agriculture. Tlaloc was one of the chiefs of the agriculture gods. He made it rain so that crops could grow, but when he was angry he could create violent thunderstorms. He is usually portrayed with huge jaguar fangs and rings around his eyes. His wife was Chalchiuhtlicue.

Why Did the Aztecs Fall?

Sometimes we hear the story that the Aztec Empire fell because they thought Cortés was a god. The story says that a small Spanish band of soldiers came in to meet with the Aztec emperor. The Spanish rode horses (then unknown to the Aztecs), and they had armor and guns. The Aztecs then assumed that Cortés was Quetzalcoatl, the creator god.

But there are good reasons to question this story. The story may not have shown up until decades after the Spanish conquest. The story may have been made up for the benefit of the Spanish royalty, to tell the Spanish king that these Aztecs were so primitive that they needed the guiding hand of the Spanish.

The reality is that the Spanish had superior weapons, including gunpowder. The Spanish were joined by thousands of warriors from neighboring tribes that hated the Aztecs. And they fought an Aztec army that had been greatly weakened by smallpox.

The beliefs and lives of Central American natives were forever changed by the invasion of European explorers. However, Mayan and Aztec myths are remembered by the modern descendants of these great people.

Right: Aztecs fight the Spanish army.

Above: The Spanish leader Hernán Cortés meets Montezuma II, the Aztec emperor, in 1519.

GLOSSARY

ASTRONOMY

The study of objects in space, such as the sun, moon, stars, and planets. The Mayans were known for their advanced study of astronomy.

CATHOLICISM

A Christian faith based on the practices of the Roman Catholic Church, based in Rome, Italy.

CENTRAL AMERICA

An area between the North American continent and the South American continent. It includes the countries of Guatemala, Belize, Honduras, El Salvador, Nicaragua, Costa Rica, and Panama. The area was once home to the Mayan and Aztec civilizations.

CHICHEN ITZA

An ancient Mayan city located in Yucatan, Mexico.

CITY-STATE

A major city, together with the area that surrounds it, that forms its own independent state.

HERNÁN CORTÉS

A Spanish conquistador (1485–1547) who led his troops and conquered the Aztec Empire in 1519-1521.

JAGUAR

A large, powerful cat found mainly in the forests of Central and South America. Some Mayan and Aztec gods took the form of the jaguar.

Jaguar

MONTEZUMA II

The last emperor of the Aztecs who lived from 1466-1520. He and his people were conquered by the Spanish in 1519-1521.

POPOL VUH

A book containing the Mayan creation story.

Quetzalcoatl as a feathered serpent.

QUETZALCOATL

The Aztec creator god.

SMALLPOX

An often deadly disease. The Spanish unknowingly brought the virus with them to the New World, where people had no immunity to it.

TENOCHTITLÁN

The capital of the Aztec Empire, now within Mexico City.

XIBALBA

The Mayan underworld.

INDEX

A

Ah Puch 13
Aztec Empire 18, 19, 28
Aztecs 4, 18, 19, 20, 22,
    24, 27, 28
Aztlan 22

C

Catholicism 10
Central America 4, 6, 10,
    14, 24
Chac 14
Chalchiuhtlicue 27
city-states 18
Cortés, Hernán 19, 28

E

eagle 22
Earth 14, 20

F

Flying Scab 8

G

Gathered Blood 8
Guatemala 6

H

Haab Calendar 16
Hollywood 16
Honduras 6

I

Itzamna 12, 16

J

jaguar 14, 26, 27

K

Kinich-Ahau 14

L

Long Count Calendar 16
Lord of the Smoking
    Mirror (*see*
    Tezcatlipoca)

M

Mayans 4, 6, 8, 10, 12,
    16, 18
Mexico 6, 18, 22
Mexico City 22

P

Pauahtun 15
Place of the Sun (*see*
    Tonatiuhichan)
Popol Vuh 10
Pus Demon 8

Q

Quetzalcoatl 20, 24, 25,
    26, 28

S

sacrifice, human 20
smallpox 19, 28

T

Tenochtitlán 18, 22
Texcoco, Lake 22
Tezcatlipoca 20, 26
Tlaloc 27
Toltecs 22
Tonatiuhichan 20
Tzolk'in Calendar 16

W

Wisconsin 22
Woman of the Jade Skirt
    (*see* Chalchiuhtlicue)

X

Xibalba 8
Xolotl 25

Y

Yucatán Peninsula 6